Urban Art

- Hanging Art 6
- Art in Town Parks 8
- Cool Cows 10
- Art and Light 12
- Is It Art? 16

SCHOLASTIC

Published in the UK by
Scholastic Education, 2024
Scholastic Distribution Centre, Bosworth Avenue,
Tournament Fields, Warwick, CV34 6UQ
Scholastic Ireland, 89E Lagan Road, Dublin Industrial
Estate, Glasnevin, Dublin, D11 HP5F

SCHOLASTIC and associated logos are trademarks
and/or registered trademarks of Scholastic Inc.
www.scholastic.co.uk

© 2024 Scholastic

1 2 3 4 5 6 7 8 9   4 5 6 7 8 9 0 1 2 3

Printed by Ashford Colour Press

This book is made of materials from
well-managed, FSC®-certified forests and
other controlled sources.

A CIP catalogue record for this book is available from
the British Library.

ISBN 978-0702-32719-3

All rights reserved. This book is sold subject to
the condition that it shall not, by way of trade or
otherwise, be lent, hired out or otherwise
circulated in any form of binding or cover other than
that in which it is published. No part of
this publication may be reproduced, stored in
a retrieval system, or transmitted in any form
or by any other means (electronic, mechanical,
photocopying, recording or otherwise) without
prior written permission of Scholastic.

Every effort has been made to trace copyright
holders for the works reproduced in this
publication, and the publishers apologise for any
inadvertent omissions.

Author
Abbie Rushton

Editorial team
Rachel Morgan, Vicki Yates, Sasha Morton
and Alison Gilbert

Design team
Dipa Mistry, Andrea Lewis and We Are Grace

Photographs
Cover (grafitti) Elymas /Shutterstock
Cover (road) sorendls/iStock
Cover (wall texture) Wylius/iStock
p4–5 Dusan Stankovic/iStock
p6, 16 paul rushton/Shutterstock
p6 (background) Krushevskaya/Shutterstock
p7 Catalin Lazar/Shutterstock
p8, 16 sunsinger/Shutterstock
p8–9 (background) ganjalex/Shutterstock
p9 Armando Oliveira/Shutterstock
p10, 16 Oksana Ku/Shutterstock
p1, 10–11, 16 (background) AlexanderTrou/
Shutterstock
p11 Eillen/iStock
p12, 16 Zhukova Valentyna/Shutterstock
p13 (mirrors) Zhank0/Shutterstock
p13 (background) ganjalex/Shutterstock
p14–15 Mehaniq/Shutterstock

How to use this book

This book practises these letters and letter sounds:

| ar (as in 'art') | or (as in 'for') | ow (as in 'cow') |
| air (as in 'pair') | er (as in 'ladder') | |

Here are some of the words in the book that use the sounds above:

yarn   town   patterns   form

This book uses these common tricky words:

the   they   go   and   you

Before reading

- Read the title and look at the cover. Discuss what the book might be about.

During reading

- If necessary, sound out and then blend the sounds to read the word: g-ar-d-e-n, garden.
- Pause every so often to talk about the information.

After reading

- Talk about what has been read. Look at page 16 and discuss the images shown.

This book looks at urban art in towns.

This pair need ladders.

Hanging Art

This yarn art hangs in a town garden.

This vivid parasol art hangs in the air.

Art in Town Parks

This art form has six silver parts.

They go in at night.

Cool Cows

Cow art has been popping up in towns for years.

Look at the patterns.

Art and Light

Art lights up this dark garden.

Art in the air shimmers in the light.

Is It Art?

Is this art or mess?

You pick!

Urban Art

Hanging Art p6

Art in Town Parks p8

Cool Cows p10

Art and Light p12

Is It Art? p16